BACH
FLUTE SOLOS

To access audio visit:
www.halleonard.com/mylibrary

Enter Code
2872-1942-9281-7022

Recording credit:
Piano and harpsichord accompaniments by David Pearl

Cherry Lane Music Company
Director of Publications/Project Editor: Mark Phillips

ISBN 978-1-60378-389-7

Visit Hal Leonard Online at
www.halleonard.com

Piano   Harpsichord

Sonata in E-flat Major, BWV 1031

2nd Movement "Siciliano"

by Johann Sebastian Bach

FLUTE

Sonata in A Major, BWV 1032
2nd Movement "Largo"

by Johann Sebastian Bach

FLUTE

Slowly

Sonata in C Major, BWV 1033
2nd Movement "Allegro"

by Johann Sebastian Bach

Piano   Harpsichord

FLUTE

Moderately fast

Sonata in C Major, BWV 1033

4th Movement "Menuetto I & II"

by Johann Sebastian Bach

2nd time, D.C. (no repeats) al Fine

9

Piano   Harpsichord

Sonata in E Minor, BWV 1034

2nd Movement "Allegro"

by Johann Sebastian Bach

FLUTE

Moderately fast

Piano   Harpsichord

Sonata in E Minor, BWV 1034
3rd Movement "Andante"

by Johann Sebastian Bach

FLUTE

Moderately

Sonata in E Major, BWV 1035

2nd Movement "Allegro"

by Johann Sebastian Bach

FLUTE

Moderately fast

17

Orchestral Suite No. 2
in B Minor, BWV 1067
"Sarabande"

by Johann Sebastian Bach

FLUTE

Orchestral Suite No. 2
in B Minor, BWV 1067
"Rondeau"

by Johann Sebastian Bach

FLUTE

Moderately, in 2

Orchestral Suite No. 2
in B Minor, BWV 1067
"Badinerie"

by Johann Sebastian Bach

Piano   **Harpsichord**

FLUTE

Moderately fast

Piano   Harpsichord

Sonata in C Major, BWV 1033
3rd Movement "Adagio"

by Johann Sebastian Bach

FLUTE

Slowly